From
Judy
12/2025

Published 2024

FiNGERPRINT!

An imprint of Prakash Books India Pvt. Ltd

113/A, Darya Ganj,
New Delhi-110 002
Email: info@prakashbooks.com/sales@prakashbooks.com

 Fingerprint Publishing
 @FingerprintP
 @fingerprintpublishingbooks
www.fingerprintpublishing.com

ISBN: 978 93 5856 487 7

To . . . .

From . . . .

Hey, fabulous YOU!

Let's embrace your inner sparkle because guess what?

YOU ARE BEAUTIFUL!

We all have a charm that can light up a room and a personality that shines bright like a diamond.

Embrace those quirks, those flaws, and those traits, and celebrate the beauty of being uniquely YOU.

Because you are beautiful in your own imperfect perfect way!

"Look around.
Look at what we have.
Beauty is everywhere—you
only have to look to see it."

BOB ROSS

"IF ROSES COULD TALK,
THEY WOULD NOT BOAST
OF THEIR BEAUTY, BECAUSE
THEY KNOW THAT THEY HAVE
ALWAYS BEEN BEAUTIFUL."

Michael Bassey Johnson

"Forgive yourself for believing that you're anything less than beautiful."

IYANLA VANZANT

"When you don't feel beautiful,
look at your true reflection.
You are a miracle made out
of stars, my love, you are
stardust perfection."

CHRISTY ANN MARTINE

"You are a beautiful
and wonderful soul.
Recognize and illuminate it."

LAILAH GIFTY AKITA

"There is a kind of beauty
in imperfection."

CONRAD HALL

"Be who you are and say what you feel, because those who mind don't matter, and those who matter don't mind."

BERNARD M. BARUCH

"The real sin
against life is to abuse
and destroy beauty,
even one's own– even more,
one's own, for that has been
put in our care, and we
are responsible for
its preservation."

KATHERINE
ANNE PORTER

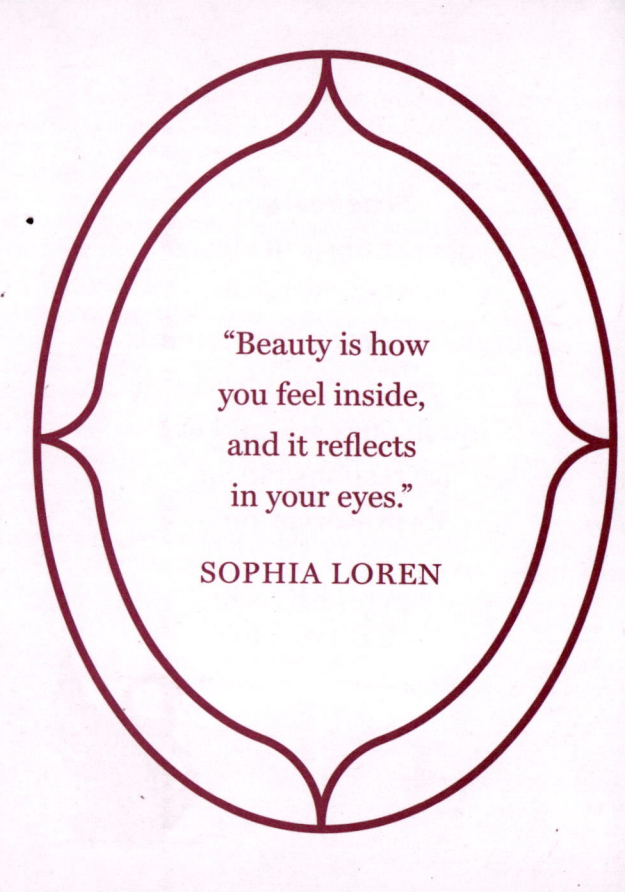

"Beauty is how
you feel inside,
and it reflects
in your eyes."

SOPHIA LOREN

"The best way to be original is to be yourself."

EVAN SPIEGEL

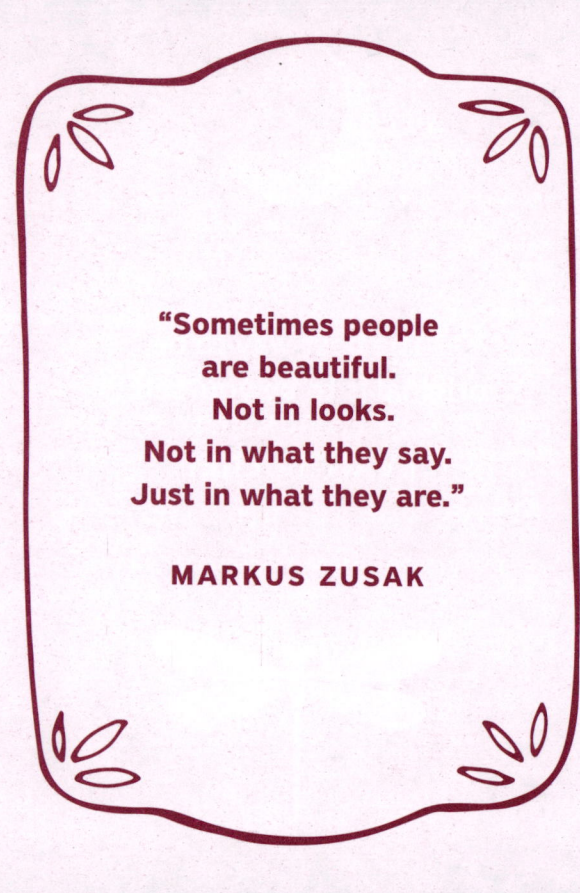

"Sometimes people
are beautiful.
Not in looks.
Not in what they say.
Just in what they are."

MARKUS ZUSAK

"YES, YOU ARE BEAUTIFUL!
YOU ARE MAGICAL BECAUSE
OF ALL YOUR FLAWS,
QUIRKS, AND WEIRDNESS!
YES, YOU ARE BEAUTIFUL
IN YOUR OWN UNIQUE WAY."

Avijeet Das

"You are beautiful
when you are happy."

OSCAR WILDE

"Life is beautiful
and so are you."

DEBASISH MRIDHA

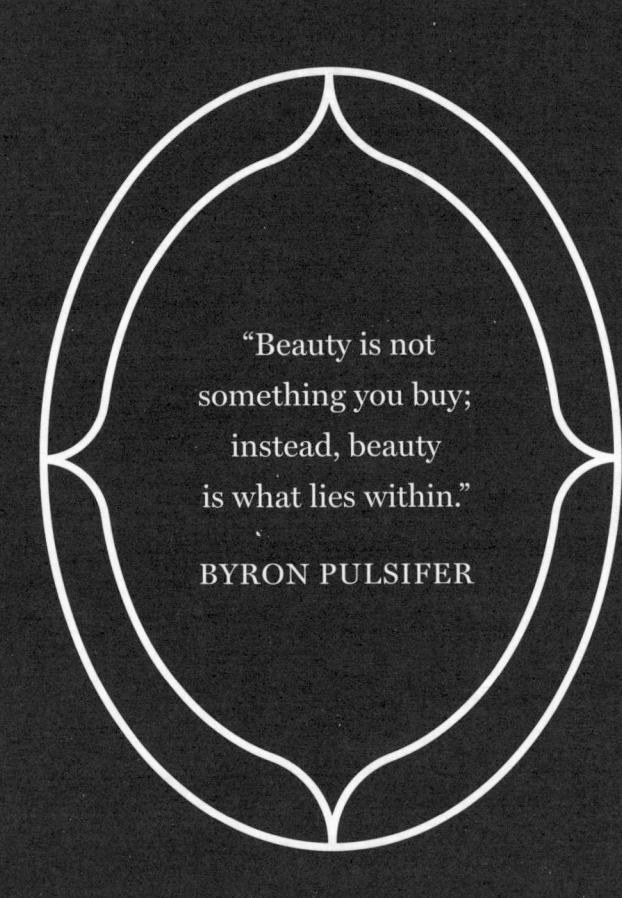

"Beauty is not
something you buy;
instead, beauty
is what lies within."

BYRON PULSIFER

"It's that heart of gold
and stardust soul
that makes you beautiful."

R.M. BRODERICK

"If people were more concerned
with how they looked on the inside,
then on the outside, the world
would be a nicer place to exist."

DAVID WALSH

"You are beautiful because you say you are, and you hold yourself that way."

MARY LAMBERT

"JUST EXACTLY AS YOU ARE,
THIS MINUTE, RIGHT NOW,
WITHOUT CHANGING A THING . . .
YOU ARE BEAUTIFUL.
BEAUTIFUL ENOUGH TO TAKE
GOD'S BREATH AWAY. . ."

Neale Donald Walsch

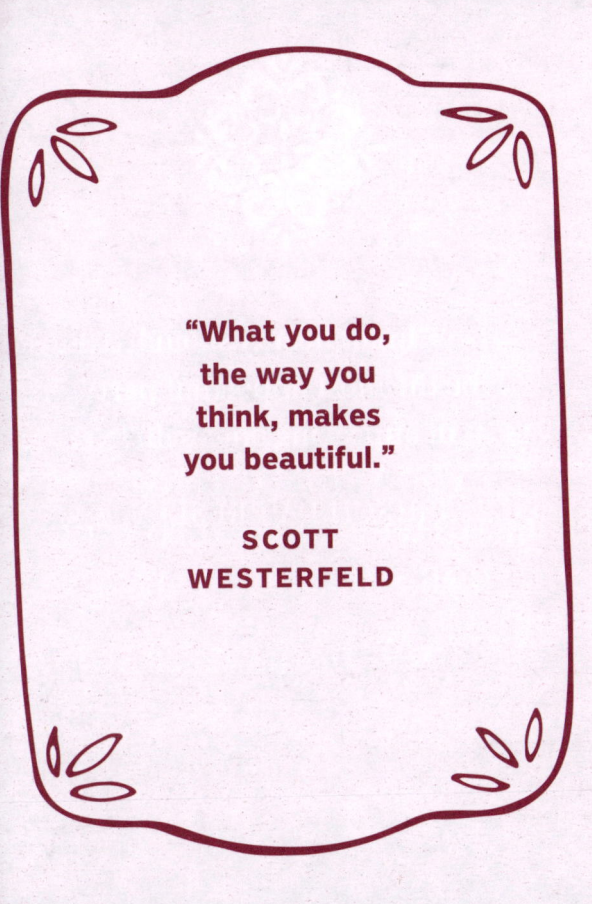

"What you do,
the way you
think, makes
you beautiful."

**SCOTT
WESTERFELD**

"Inner beauty should
be the most important part
of improving one's self."

PRISCILLA PRESLEY

"You are worthy
of love and respect.
You are beautiful,
gifted, and intelligent.
Don't let the storm
make you forget it."

RUSSELL T. DAVIES

"It is better to be hated for what you are than to be loved for what you are not."

ANDRÉ GIDE

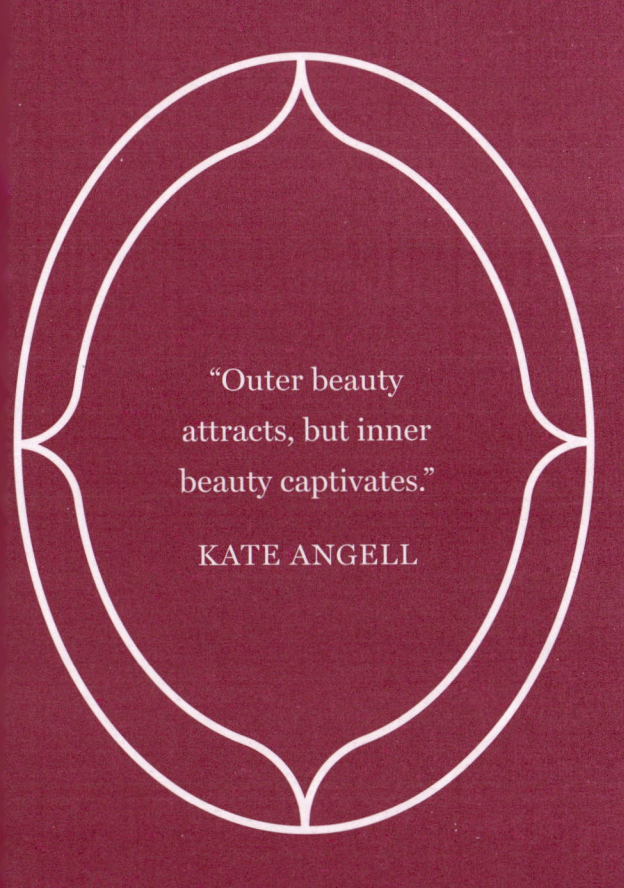

"Outer beauty
attracts, but inner
beauty captivates."

KATE ANGELL

"Beauty is about
enhancing what you have.
Let yourself shine through."

JANELLE MONAE

"FOLLOW YOUR HEART,
LISTEN TO YOUR INNER VOICE,
STOP CARING ABOUT WHAT
OTHERS THINK."

Roy T. Bennett

"True beauty is when
someone radiates that
they like themselves."

AIMEE MULLINS

"Beauty lives with kindness."

WILLIAM SHAKESPEARE

"Let your inner beauty be your main force."

ANOIR OU-CHAD

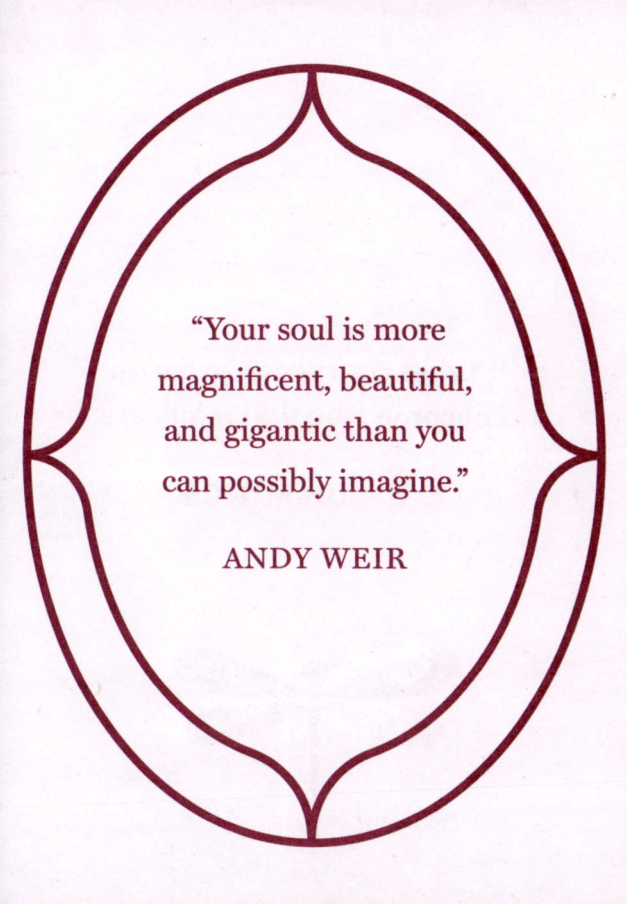

"Your soul is more magnificent, beautiful, and gigantic than you can possibly imagine."

ANDY WEIR

"It takes courage to grow up and become who you really are."

E.E. CUMMINGS

"Love yourself for who you are. You are beautiful inside and out, and nobody can take that away from you."

CHRISTINA MILIAN

"You're a beautiful flower,
fall fearlessly."

AKASH S. BANSAL

"Beauty is really all
about confidence.
If you feel beautiful,
then you are beautiful."

SOFIA VERGARA

"When beauty lives in the heart,
it doesn't need to show up
anywhere else."

STEVE GOODIER

"You are beautiful because you let yourself feel, and that is a brave thing indeed."

SHINJI MOON

"Not much to look at, but
as with all true beauty,
it is what's inside
that counts."

MATT SEWELL

"BEAUTY IS DEFINED NOT BY
OUR PHYSICAL APPEARANCE
BUT BY WHO WE CHOOSE TO BE."

Andrew Davenport

"Follow your inner moonlight;
don't hide the madness."

ALLEN GINSBERG

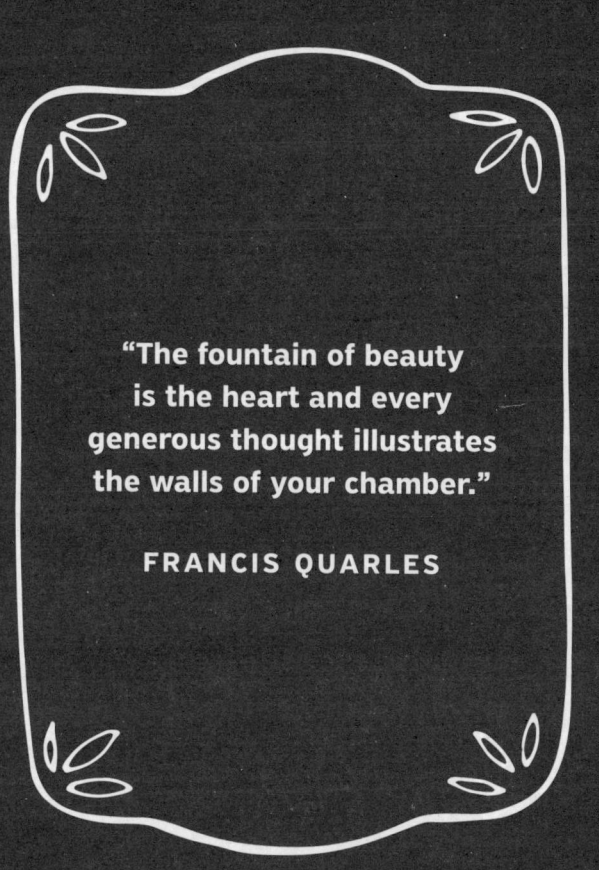

"The fountain of beauty
is the heart and every
generous thought illustrates
the walls of your chamber."

FRANCIS QUARLES

"Groom yourself with a comb
of confidence and inner beauty."

SUYASHA SUBEDI

"PRETTY IS SOMETHING
YOU'RE BORN WITH.
BUT BEAUTIFUL,
THAT'S AN EQUAL
OPPORTUNITY ADJECTIVE."

Ralph Waldo Emerson

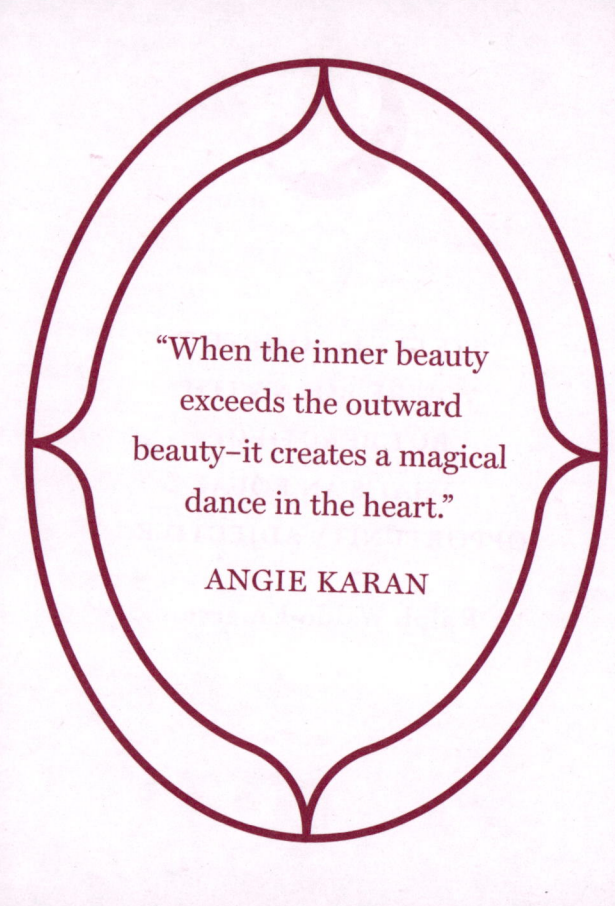

"When the inner beauty exceeds the outward beauty–it creates a magical dance in the heart."

ANGIE KARAN

"Be your own celebrity.
Chase your own self.
You are worth infinite
treasures of this planet."

HIRAL NAGDA

"Focus on your inner beauty. Outer beauty will draw people to you, inner beauty will keep them in your presence."

ROBERT OVERSTREET

"The beauty that we find
in the world is a reflection
of the beauty inside of us."

ABHIJIT NASKAR

"Your inner light is what makes you beautiful."

MARY DAVIS

"It's all about embracing your inner beauty and just living for yourself."

MELANIE BROWN

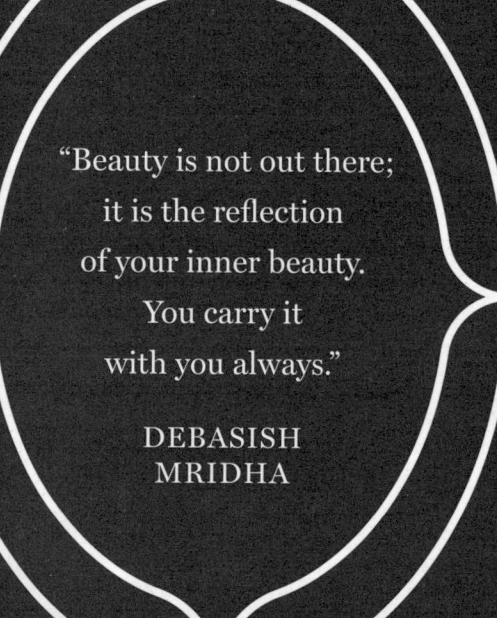

"Beauty is not out there;
it is the reflection
of your inner beauty.
You carry it
with you always."

DEBASISH
MRIDHA

"Beauty begins the moment
you decide to be yourself."

COCO CHANEL

"You are beautiful.
You are strong.
You are worth it.
You are loved."

MACAILE HUTT

A FRIENDLY REMINDER!

Beauty comes in all shapes, colors, and sizes. Societal standards don't determine your worth, nor do other people's opinions. The most radiant beauty is the confidence that shines because of self-acceptance and self-love.

So, stand tall and embrace your individuality. Believe in yourself and cherish your inner beauty.

With that amazing smile of yours, do the world a favor and illuminate everything around you!

"YOU ARE MORE POWERFUL THAN YOU KNOW; YOU ARE BEAUTIFUL JUST AS YOU ARE."

Melissa Etheridge

"Try your hardest to be confident in who you are. You are enough, you are beautiful."

MEAGAN TANDY

"You were born an original.
Don't die a copy."

JOHN MASON

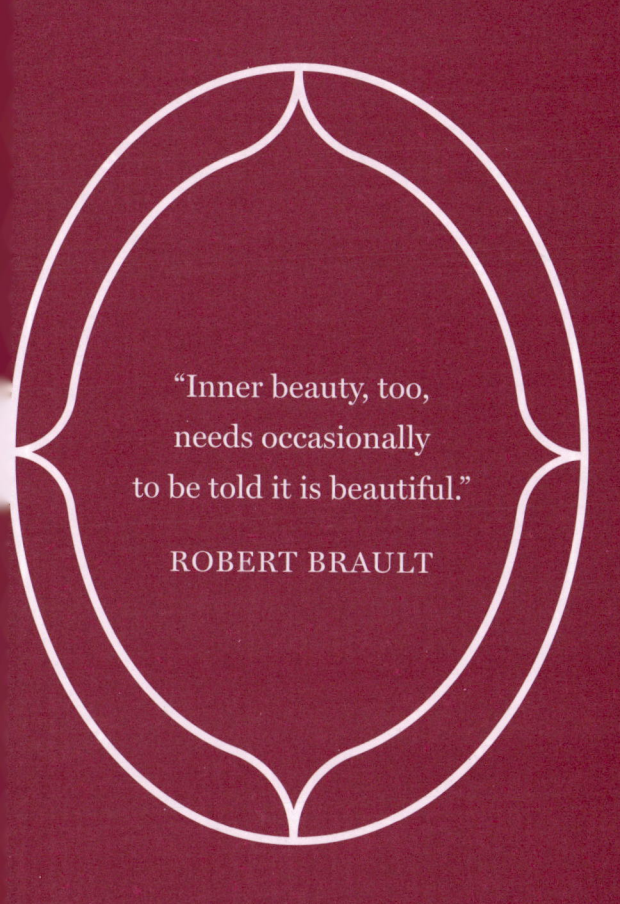

"Inner beauty, too,
needs occasionally
to be told it is beautiful."

ROBERT BRAULT

"It is the beauty within us that makes it possible for us to recognize the beauty around us. The question is not what you look at, but what you see."

HENRY DAVID THOREAU

"Beauty is power;
a smile is its sword."

JOHN RAY

"People often say that beauty is in the eye of the beholder, and I say that the most liberating thing about beauty is realising you are the beholder."

SALMA HAYEK

"You're beautiful.
Don't let anyone
tell you otherwise."

ANONYMOUS

"Beauty is eternity gazing
at itself in a mirror."

KHALIL GIBRAN

"SO MANY THINGS BECOME
BEAUTIFUL WHEN YOU
REALLY LOOK."

Lauren Oliver

"A swan is beautiful, even
if mocked by ugly ducks."

MATSHONA DHLIWAYO

"Outer beauty is inner beauty made visible, and it manifests itself in the light that flows in our eyes."

PAULO COELHO

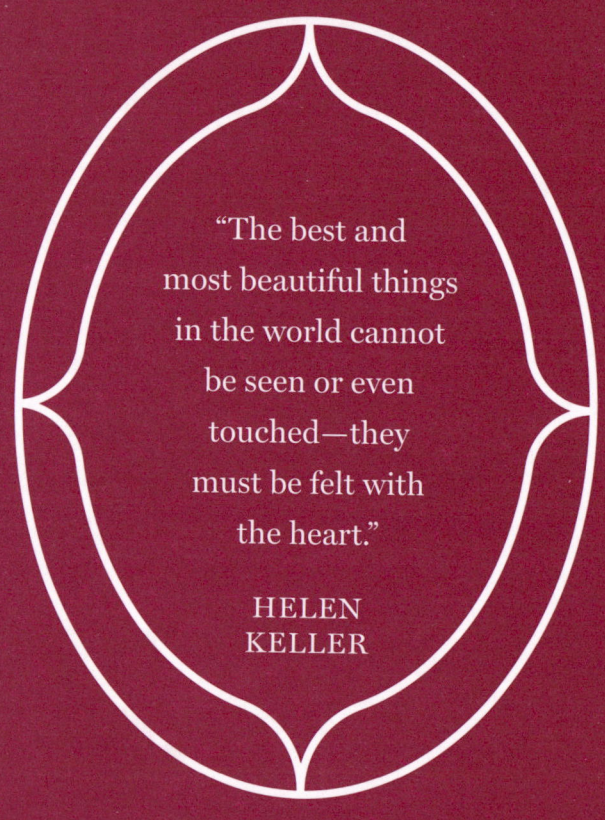

"The best and
most beautiful things
in the world cannot
be seen or even
touched—they
must be felt with
the heart."

HELEN
KELLER

"Always be a first-rate
version of yourself,
instead of a second-rate
version of somebody else."

JUDY GARLAND

"You are good enough, smart enough, beautiful enough, strong enough."

LOLLY DASKAL

"THE ABSENCE
OF FLAW IN BEAUTY
IS ITSELF A FLAW."

Havelock Ellis

"To be beautiful means
to be yourself.
You don't need to be
accepted by others.
You need to accept yourself."

THICH NHAT HANH

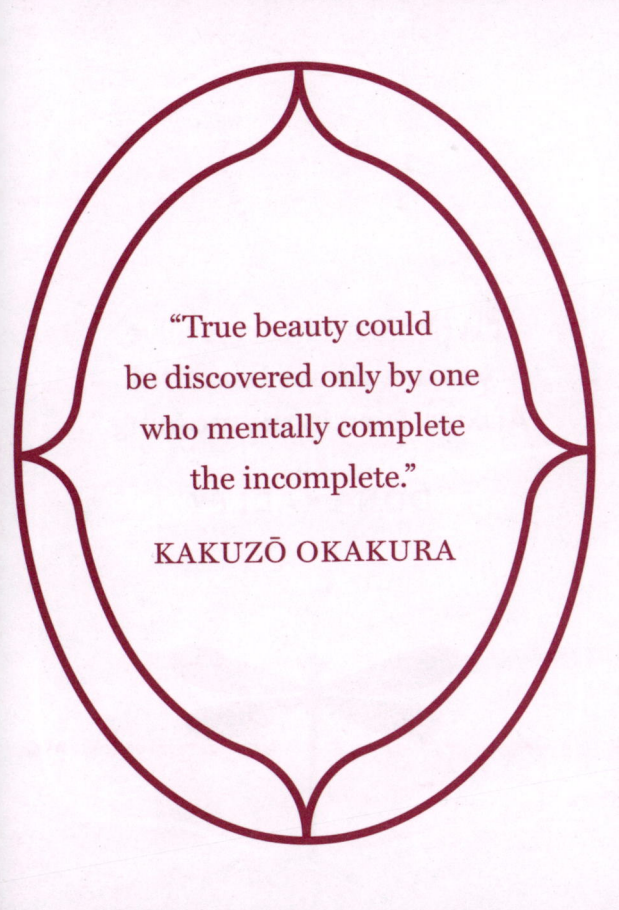

"True beauty could
be discovered only by one
who mentally complete
the incomplete."

KAKUZŌ OKAKURA

"When your heart is alive,
you are always beautiful.
Always. Even in the morning."

DON BRADLEY

"Our hearts are drunk
with a beauty our eyes
could never see."

GEORGE W.
RUSSELL

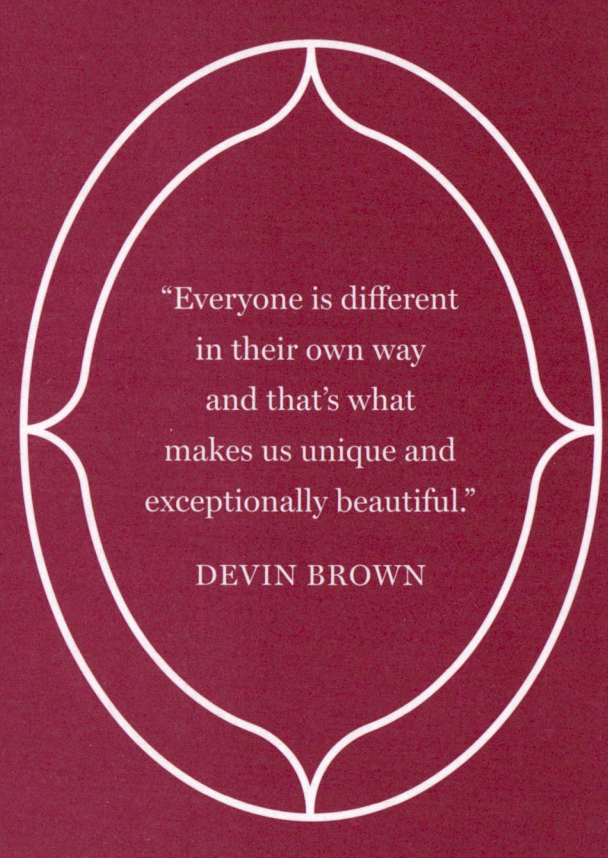

"Everyone is different
in their own way
and that's what
makes us unique and
exceptionally beautiful."

DEVIN BROWN

"Angels only care about what
you look like on the inside.
A pure heart is a vessel that
contains a soul's true beauty."

MOLLY FRIEDENFELD

"EMBRACE YOUR
OWN PERSONAL BEAUTY.
LOVE WHO YOU ARE TODAY
AND EVERYDAY."

Robert Jones

"The seeds of beauty
are in humility."

MAXIME
LAGACÉ

"If you realized how
beautiful you are,
you would fall at
your own feet."

BYRON KATIE

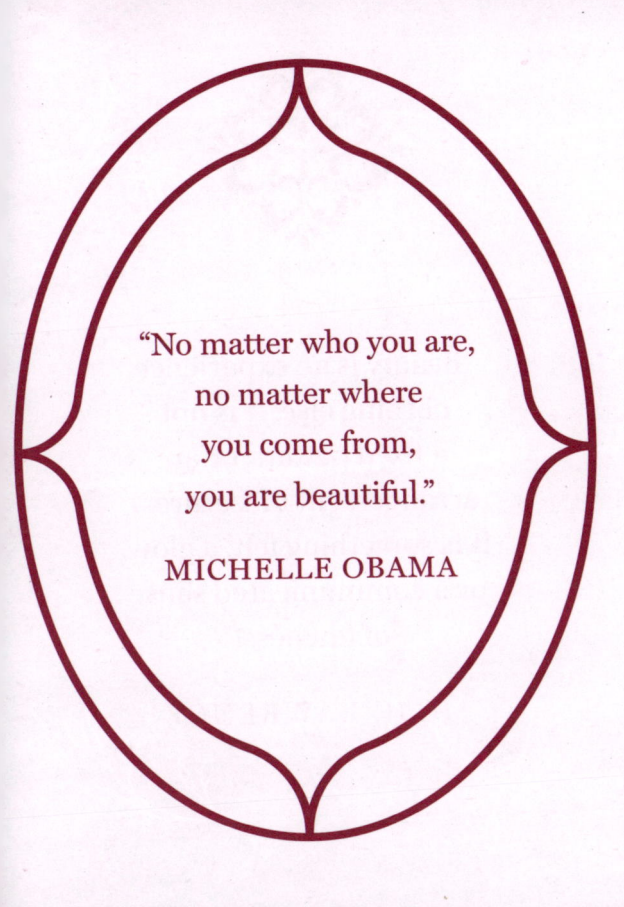

"No matter who you are,
no matter where
you come from,
you are beautiful."

MICHELLE OBAMA

"Beauty is an experience,
nothing else. It is not
a fixed pattern or an
arrangement of features.
It is something felt, a glow,
or a communicated sense
of fineness."

D. H. LAWRENCE

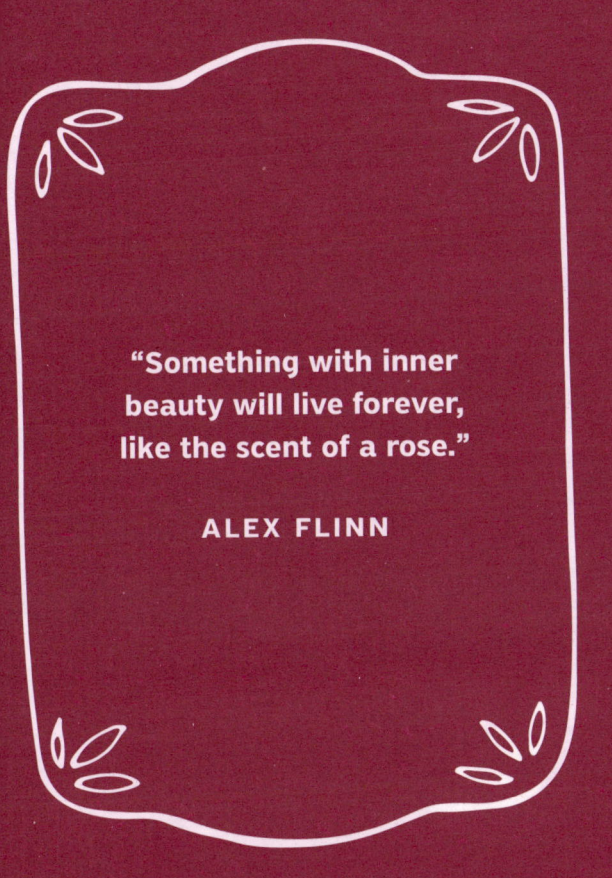

"Something with inner beauty will live forever, like the scent of a rose."

ALEX FLINN

"Embrace the uniqueness
that makes you, you."

BRENDON BURCHARD

"Beauty is a radiance that
originates from within
and comes from inner security
and strong character."

JANE SEYMOUR

"YOU ARE ONE THING ONLY.
YOU ARE A DIVINE BEING.
AN ALL-POWERFUL CREATOR."

Anthon St. Maarten

"Whenever you are creating beauty around you, you are restoring your own soul."

ALICE WALKER

"YOU'RE ABSOLUTELY GORGEOUS.
AND THAT'S THE LEAST
INTERESTING THING
ABOUT YOU."

Anonymous

"There is certainly no absolute
standard of beauty.
That precisely is what makes
its pursuit so interesting."

JOHN KENNETH
GALBRAITH

"There is nothing that makes its way more directly to the soul than beauty."

JOSEPH ADDISON

"Every time you smile at someone,
it is an action of love, a gift to that
person, a beautiful thing."

MOTHER TERESA

"A pure heart is superlatively rare
and even more attractive."

J.S.B. MORSE

"Beauty is in the heart
of the beholder."

H. G. WELLS

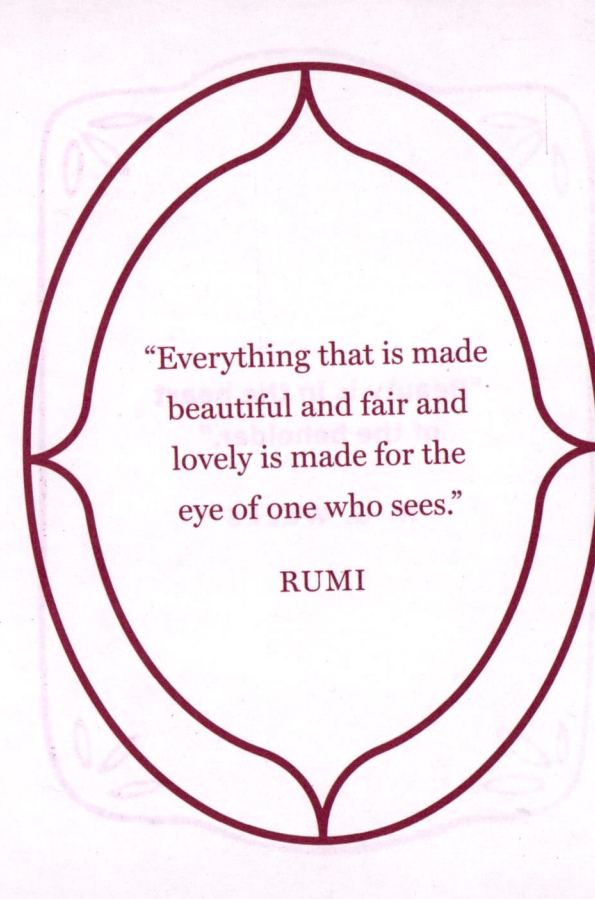

"Everything that is made
beautiful and fair and
lovely is made for the
eye of one who sees."

RUMI

"As we open our hearts to others,
we begin to discover the
truth of our own inner beauty,
inner strength, and inner light."

SUSAN JEFFERS

"The power of finding beauty
in the humblest things makes
the home happy and life lovely."

LOUISA MAY ALCOTT

"Think of all the beauty still left around you and be happy."

ANNE FRANK

"WHEN YOU REACH THE HEART
OF LIFE YOU SHALL FIND
BEAUTY IN ALL THINGS,
EVEN IN THE EYES THAT
ARE BLIND TO BEAUTY."

Khalil Gibran

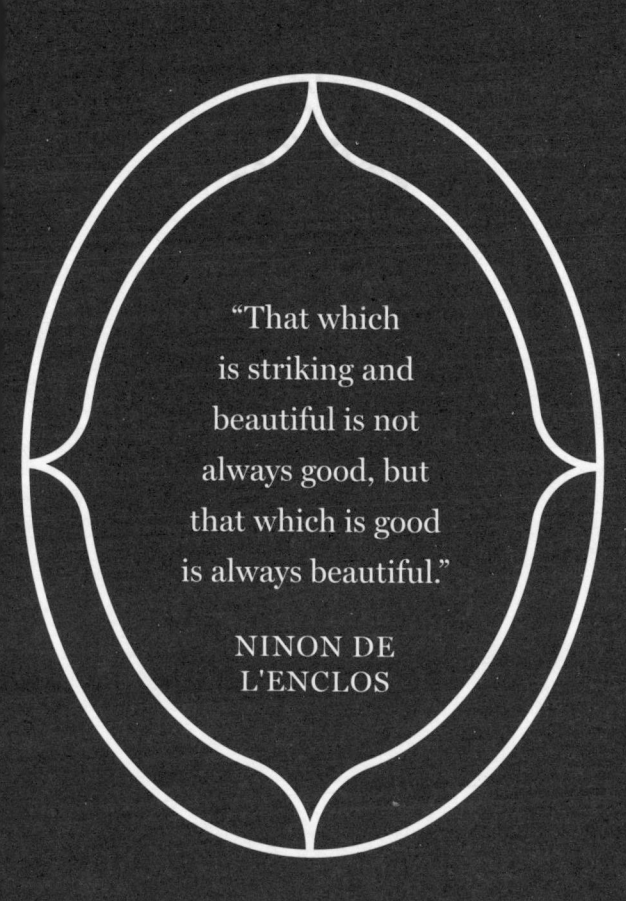

"That which
is striking and
beautiful is not
always good, but
that which is good
is always beautiful."

NINON DE
L'ENCLOS

"Nothing can dim the light
which shines from within."

MAYA ANGELOU

"Though we travel the world
over to find the beautiful,
we must carry it with
us or we find it not."

RALPH WALDO
EMERSON

"BEAUTY PLEASES
THE EYES ONLY;
SWEETNESS OF DISPOSITION
CHARMS THE SOUL."

Voltaire

"When you are content
to be simply yourself and
don't compare or compete,
everyone will respect you."

LAO TZU

"The best part of beauty is that which no picture can express."

FRANCIS BACON

"Beauty is no quality
in things themselves:
it exists merely
in the mind which
contemplates them;
and each mind perceives
a different beauty."

DAVID HUME

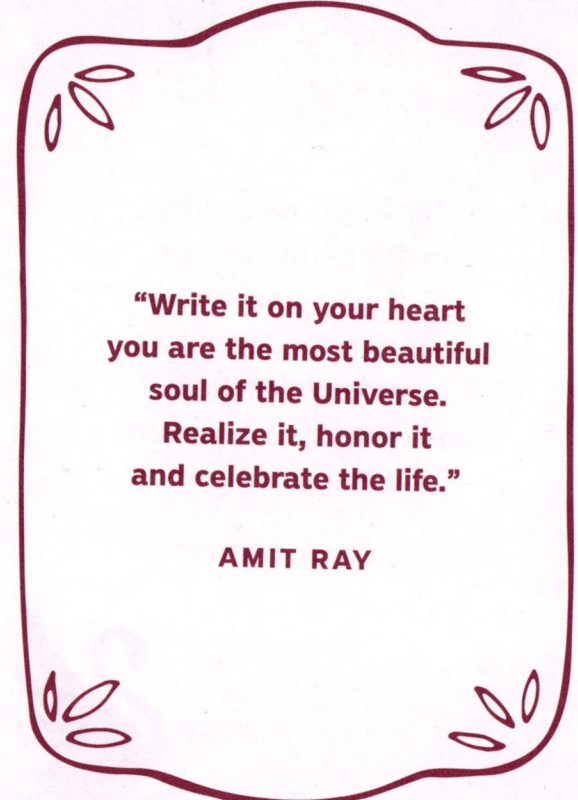

"Write it on your heart
you are the most beautiful
soul of the Universe.
Realize it, honor it
and celebrate the life."

AMIT RAY

"You are beautiful.
Your beauty, just like your
capacity for life, happiness,
and success, is immeasurable."

STEVE MARABOLI

"You're beautiful.
You'd have to work pretty
hard to mess that up."

JENNIFER ECHOLS

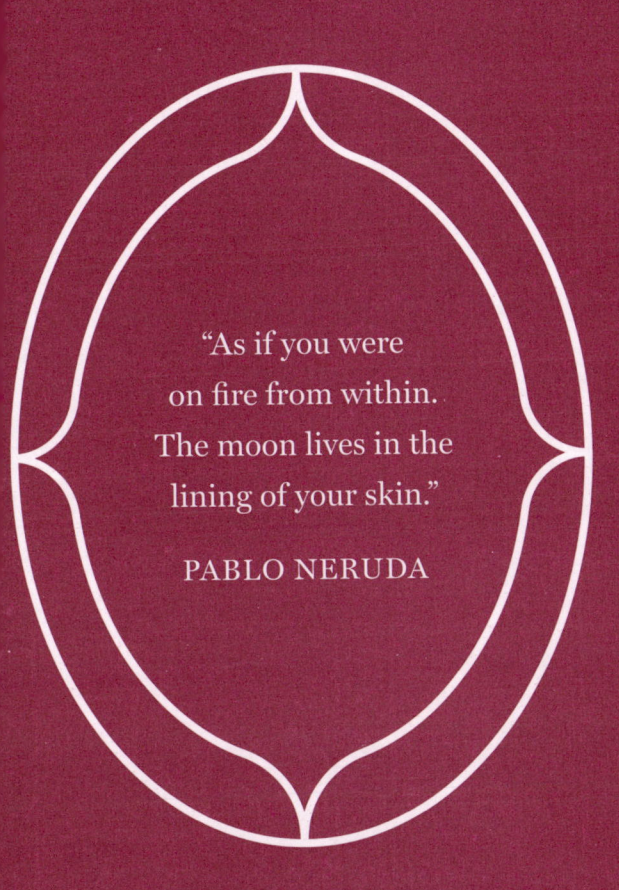

"As if you were
on fire from within.
The moon lives in the
lining of your skin."

PABLO NERUDA

"YOU HAVE TO RELY
ON WHATEVER SPARK
YOU HAVE INSIDE."

Lisa Kleypas

"Inner beauty is what makes
a person's outer beauty
exquisitely beautiful."

ANONYMOUS

"You are beautiful, and your worth is not defined by your appearance."

VIOLA DAVIS

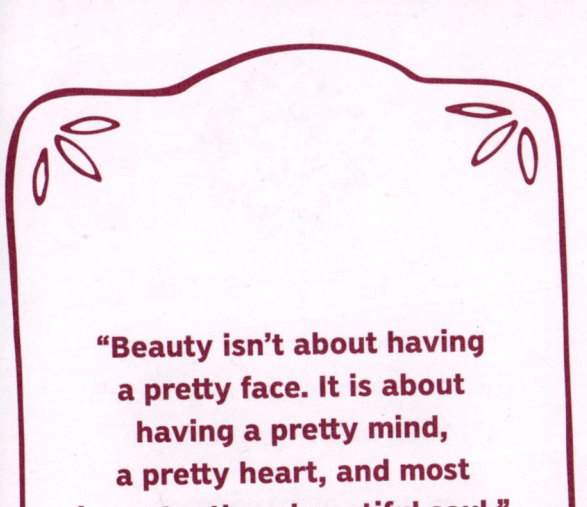

"Beauty isn't about having a pretty face. It is about having a pretty mind, a pretty heart, and most importantly, a beautiful soul."

ANONYMOUS

"The more you like yourself,
the less you are like anyone else,
which makes you unique."

WALT DISNEY

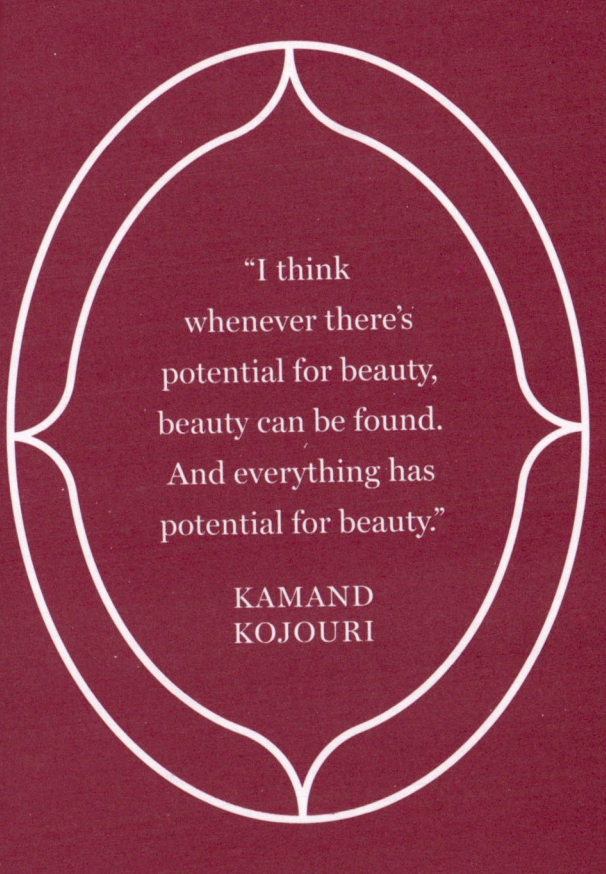

"I think
whenever there's
potential for beauty,
beauty can be found.
And everything has
potential for beauty."

KAMAND
KOJOURI

"LIVE QUIETLY IN THE
MOMENT AND SEE THE
BEAUTY OF ALL BEFORE YOU.
THE FUTURE WILL TAKE
CARE OF ITSELF. . ."

PARAMAHANSA
YOGANANDA

"Since love grows within you,
so beauty grows.
For love is the beauty
of the soul."

SAINT AUGUSTINE

"The most beautiful things you can wear are your self-confidence and your self-love."

LETICIA RAE

"You are beautiful
like a rainbow after the storm."

CARA DELEVINGNE

"Wisdom is the abstract
of the past, but
beauty is the promise
of the future."

OLIVER WENDELL
HOLMES

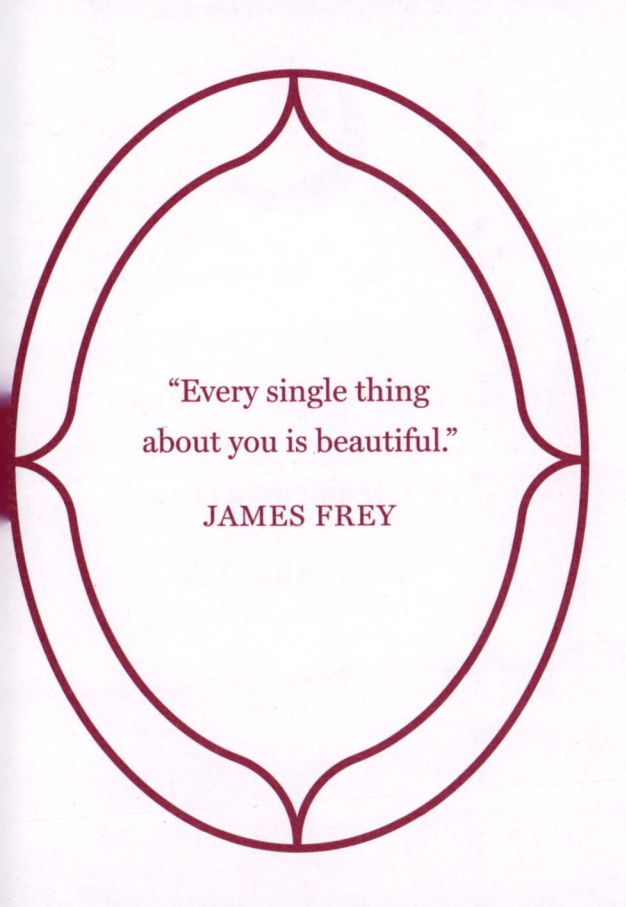

"Every single thing
about you is beautiful."

JAMES FREY

"THERE IS NO EXQUISITE BEAUTY . . .
WITHOUT SOME STRANGENESS
IN THE PROPORTION."

Edgar Allan Poe

"Beauty is a fragile gift."

OVID

"Be yourself.
Above all, let who you are,
what you are, what you believe,
shine through every sentence
you write, every piece you finish."

JOHN JAKES

"Take care of you inner,
spiritual beauty.
That will reflect
in your face."

DOLORES DEL RIO

"A thing of beauty
is a joy forever."

JOHN KEATS

"Let today be the day you stand strong in the truth of your beauty. Journey through your day without attachment to the validation of others."

STEVE MARABOLI

"You are beautiful because
of the light you carry inside you."

SUSAN POLIS SCHUTZ

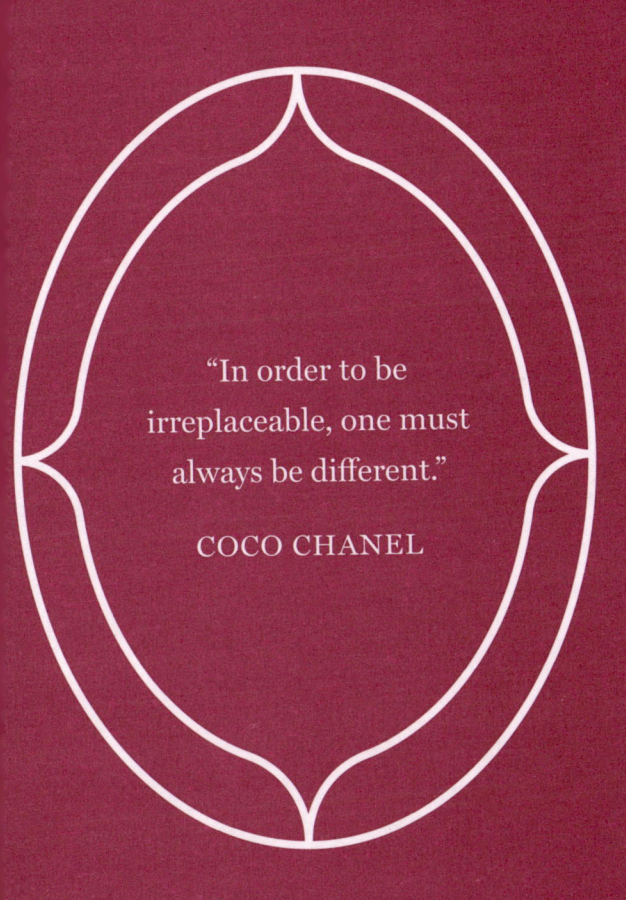

"In order to be irreplaceable, one must always be different."

COCO CHANEL

"YOUR SELF-WORTH IS NOT
MEASURED BY YOUR APPEARANCE,
BUT BY THE LOVE AND KINDNESS
YOU GIVE TO THE WORLD."

Karen Salmansohn

"Beauty is not caused.
It is."

EMILY
DICKINSON

"Believe in yourself
and all that you are.
Know that there
is something inside
you that is greater
than any obstacle."

CHRISTIAN D. LARSON

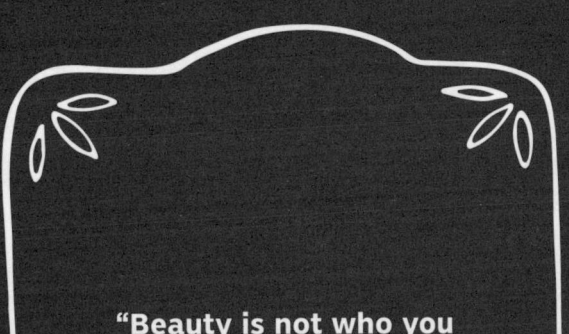

"Beauty is not who you are on the outside, it is the wisdom and time you gave away to save another struggling soul like you."

SHANNON L. ALDER

"There is in true beauty,
as in courage, something
which narrow souls
cannot dare to admire."

WILLIAM CONGREVE

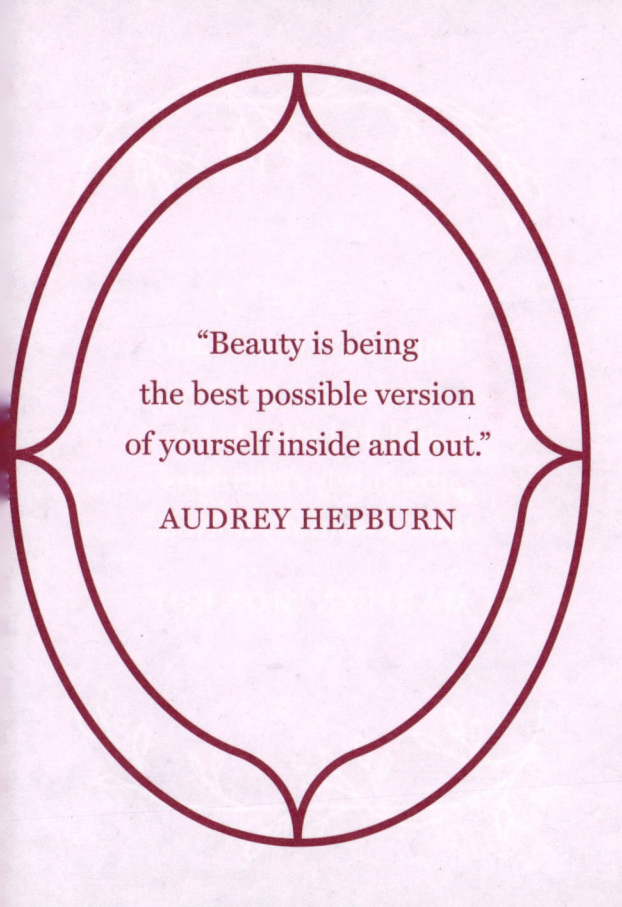

"Beauty is being
the best possible version
of yourself inside and out."

AUDREY HEPBURN

"Imperfection is beauty,
madness is genius,
and it's better to be
absolutely ridiculous
than absolutely boring."

MARILYN MONROE

"Beauty has a lot to
do with character."

KEVYN AUCOIN

"Of all the things that you can be, choose to be kind and choose to be beautiful."

ANTHONY HINCKS

"HOW YOU LOVE
YOURSELF IS HOW
YOU TEACH OTHERS
TO LOVE YOU."

Rupi Kaur

"You are imperfect,
permanently and
inevitably flawed.
And you are beautiful."

AMY BLOOM

"If you retain nothing else, always remember the most important rule of beauty, which is: who cares?"

TINE FREY

"I believe inner beauty
is beauty in its truest form.
When we nurture ourselves,
it brings an inevitable,
positive transformation."

PAULA ABDUL

"THERE IS NO COSMETIC
FOR BEAUTY LIKE HAPPINESS."

Maria Mitchell

"And when all the wars are over,
a butterfly will still be beautiful."

RUSKIN BOND

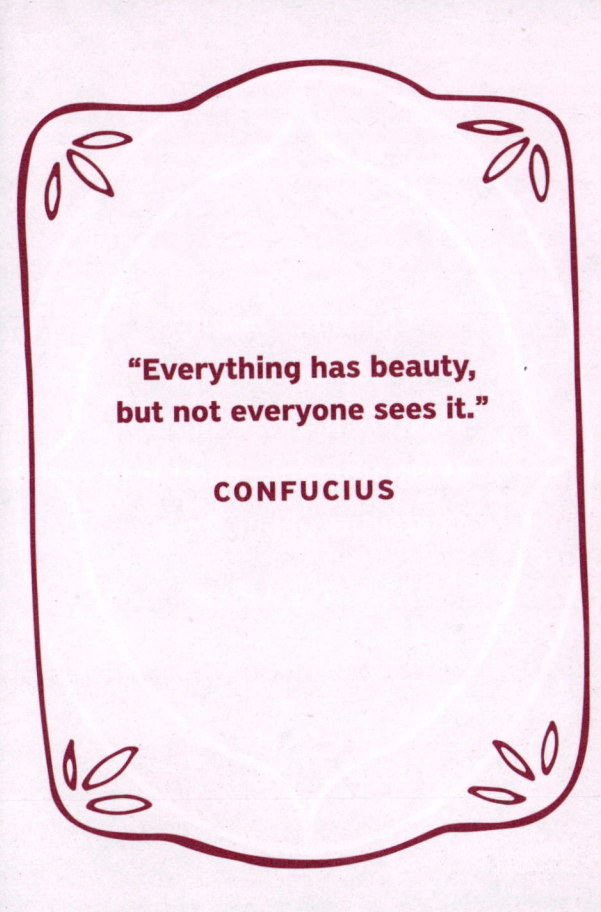

"Everything has beauty,
but not everyone sees it."

CONFUCIUS

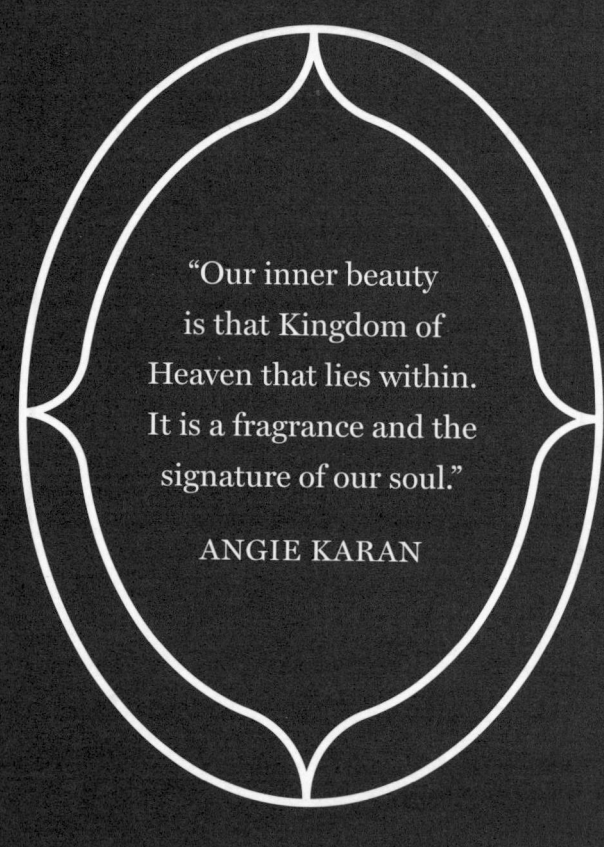

"Our inner beauty
is that Kingdom of
Heaven that lies within.
It is a fragrance and the
signature of our soul."

ANGIE KARAN

"If you feel beautiful,
then you are.
Even if you don't,
you still are."

TERRI
GUILLEMETS

"YOU YOURSELF,
AS MUCH AS ANYBODY
IN THE ENTIRE UNIVERSE,
DESERVE YOUR LOVE
AND AFFECTION."

Buddha

"At the core of your heart,
you are perfect and pure.
No one and nothing
can alter that."

AMIT RAY

"The privilege of a
lifetime is to become
who you truly are."

C.G. JUNG

"YOU ARE ENOUGH JUST AS YOU ARE. EACH EMOTION YOU FEEL, EVERYTHING IN YOUR LIFE, EVERYTHING YOU DO OR DO NOT DO . . . WHERE YOU ARE AND WHO YOU ARE RIGHT NOW IS ENOUGH. IT IS PERFECT. YOU ARE PERFECT ENOUGH."

Haemin Sunim

"Beauty is simply reality
seen with the eyes of love."

RABINDRANATH TAGORE